55 Affirmations With Self Help Activities

By

Manoj Kumar Singh

Published by Power In Me Foundation

Book Name: 55 Affirmations With Self Help Activities (Paperback)

Author: Manoj Kumar Singh

Copyright

ISBN (Paperback): 978-81-954847-1-3

ISBN (Ebook): 978-81-954847-9-9

Publisher

Power In Me Foundation, H. No. 531, MIG-21, Opp. SBI Colony, Near Subhadra Memorial Hospital, Ganiyari Road, Waidhan, District- Singrauli, Madhya Pradesh, Pin Code- 486886. Email- mpowerinme@gmail.com.

Printed at Waidhan, Singrauli, Madhya Pradesh

About Author

Manoj Kumar Singh is a multifaceted and multitalented individual. He is a life coach, motivational speaker, researcher, author, poet, publisher, podcaster, trainer and social entrepreneur. He is trustee and national president of Power In Me Foundation that works for the rights of people with rare diseases.

For his endeavors he was awarded Rex Karamveer Chakra Bronze Medal in 2019, creating awareness about Hemophilia and rare diseases. He has even won best motivational speaker award in 2019.

His life has been a continuous battle against different hardships and challenges. He was born with a rare bleeding condition called Hemophilia. And had multiple near death experiences due to it. From childhood to growing up he had witnessed traumas in life that he never shared with anyone.

But as he realised his life's purpose, he recognized the need to heel self then only he could help others. He is spiritually inclined individual and sees connection of Divine within every being. He practices meditation, mindfulness and affirmations as his spiritual exercises to keep him grounded in life. Also, these activities help him to be emotionally clear and work towards his objectives. In this book he shares his success through affirmations to raise his vibes and heal.

You can follow him on social media:

Instagram @manojkumarsingh_dilse , Facebook @MKSDilse,

Podcast@ dilse_manoj

Acknowledgement

With gratitude in my heart, I would like to thank the ever-merciful Super Consciousness. The one who created the universe and everything in it. Thank you for showering your love and blessings to me in my every life challenges.

I would like to thank mother nature for she is nurturing us and helping us heal.

I give my whole hearted gratitude to my parents, family, friends and everyone who has touched my life. For presence of each one of you had helped me evolve to be the best version of myself.

I give my gratitude to Power In Me Foundation for it has been the driving force for the new beginning in my life and life's purpose to serve the mankind.

Preface

The world is going through a tough phase where it needs as much positivity possible. But you cannot sit back and hope for others to start spreading that positive vibe. You must play your part too. This book is a combination of introduction to your inner peace with positive affirmations being the tool to achieve it.

However, you cannot achieve what you want until you start making efforts for it. Thus, this book has some activities to learn and write your own affirmations for bringing in more positivity into your life.

You alone are responsible for what you make of your life. When you build positivity into your life step by step, you raise your vibrations to a higher level. You have less suffering even though the challenges of life may remain same.

The author, himself has gone through a lot in life, facing different life challenges and near to death experiences. He has channelized his life's learnings into this book as one of the activities he does through affirmation on regular basis. This book is an attempt to give you a self-help tool that will help you become stronger from within and enjoy inner peace. And help you become the better version of yourself.

What is inner peace?

You may ask different people this same question and each will answer in their own way. Some may even find it difficult to describe what being at peace means to them. But one thing that everyone will tell is that it feels good within when you have it.

In simple terms inner peace is a state when a person remains calm even in midst of several difficulties or adversities going on in their lives. This calmness is both at psychological, physical and spiritual levels.

You can feel bliss, happiness, contentment and a sense of ease because you somewhere believe that things will turnout well in the end. This state helps you to take better decisions in life at your personal and professional levels.

When majority of people in the world can attain this level of consciousness then we will see less of pain, hatred and fight. In fact, we will see more of love, empathy and support for each other.

Talking to the Universe

Some people may laugh at the very concept of talking to the universe but those who have spiritual inclination will believe it.

Now let us observe that people who do not believe this are mostly materialistic in nature and for them success in life is defined by how much money they have acquired in their life. They want a luxuries life without caring for others. However, a spiritual person sees the real connection between all beings and the environment around him.

The environment includes trees, water bodies, sky, animals, birds, insects, humans and all the celestial bodies. This is what we also call universe. And each one of us part of it. Thus, each one is connected to it.

When you are connected to something or someone, you can talk to them. They understand your act and respond accordingly.

Even you can communicate with them with your heart, thoughts, speaking, or physical act. This is how you can also talk to the universe aka the environment around you which will respond. If you pollute, you get the pollution back deteriorating your health.

When I say talking. It does not always mean speaking alone but every act of communication which can not even be seen. Prayers and affirmations are positive ways to talk to the universe to achieve blessings from it.

What are affirmations?

The answer you give for something that is true in its support is by affirming it. It means you accept it because the fact is right. Affirmations are positive words that you speak to self and tell them to the universe that you believe it is true.

They help you mould your belief system in a positive manner and your outlook towards the life.

People use affirmations to manifest their dreams and desires coupled with their work because nothing manifests until your work for it. In fact, affirmations help you manifest it faster by building positive attitude towards your goal. You can use affirmation to get money, improve relationship, love and success in life. Always remember follow affirmation with work while you feel the emotion of already having the desire being achieved.

Positive affirmations as tool for inner peace and manifestation.

Our life is a complex journey with unpredictable events that often leads us to stagnation. This stagnation is at every realm of our life comprising health, relationships, money and psychological.

In extreme cases you loose control of your life, feel stuck and may take steps that are not right for you. The impact of negative thinking coupled with negative act will lower your productivity and block your progress.

You lose your inner peace which is shown into your decision making and life is difficult. For you it is constant struggle.

It is here the use of positive thinking in the form of daily affirmations help you to reach higher levels of your consciousness. It is at this stage your thought process becomes more positive and you start to remain calm even under stress.

Regular use of the positive affirmations helps you to revamp your thought process into positive thoughts. This helps you to manifest a lot of things and achieve in your life.

How to write affirmations?

Writing affirmations is continuation of your belief into what you wish to have in your future. But the key here is to feel it in the present while you are writing.

Here are steps to write your affirmations:

1. First put your thought on one thing that you wish to have. This could be money, love, completion of a project, health etc.
2. Feel it in the present tense. Because affirmation means something that is already done and is true.
3. Start with I or My. Because it is about you.
4. Write it short. Probably one line to three lines.
5. Make it feel realistic and achievable. It is not competition. It is to build confidence and positivity.
6. Feel them and visualize how it would feel to really have them.
7. It should be your priority that you affirm for.

Guide to using this book

This book is a guide from Divine to help people who chose to follow the spiritual path of living and celebrate divine connection between all beings. Affirmation is a great tool to realise that connection and achieve what you wish for with a positive attitude in life.

The book is a small challenge for you comprising of 55 days and 55 affirmations. Each page has one affirmation or group of small affirmations for that day. You need to read that affirmation and then reflect on it for 5 minutes while closing your eyes with deep breathing. Once you have done that you need to right your own affirmation for that day in the space given.

Please note that the affirmations work when you put your intentions into motion. So, if you desire for love then feel that love within while you are writing your affirmation. Recite your written affirmation and reflect for another 5 minutes. The overall activity for the day hardly takes 10-15 minutes in a day and can be done at the start of your day or before going to bed. Remember not to be in a hurry to finish the activity like a school assignment but enjoy the process being happy.

Special note for those people who are reading the book in electronic format. You don't need to worry just keep your diary or a notebook handy where you can write down your reflection and affirmations for each day. For best result try to focus on one thing and write one affirmation each day for it throughout the challenge duration of 55 days.

As a special gift from me, I have also given three extra affirmations for you to enjoy. Because once you have learned the positive impact of affirmations into your life you won't need to write as you will start living a mindful life that is constantly in positive affirmation aka thoughts.

I Call Upon My Inner Light

To Shine Brighter.

I Call Upon The Universe

To Guide Me

Towards My Life's Purpose.

I Call Upon My Powers

To Manifest The Miracles

I Am Born To Receive.

I Am Ready.

Reflection On Affirmation (Write Here):

I Am Love.

I Am Happiness.

I Am Healthy.

I Am Healed.

I Am Aligned

With The Universe.

I Am Deeply Rooted

With Mother Earth.

I Am Abundance.

I Am Wealth.

I Am Ready.

Reflection On Affirmation (Write Here):

I Free Myself

From

The Blocking Memories.

I Free Myself

From

The Negative Energies.

I Free Myself

From

The Unwanted Fears.

I Free Myself

From The Attachments That No Longer Serve My Higher Purpose.

I Free Myself From Everything That Restricts My Growth While I Connect Myself With Mother Earth And Universal Energy.

Reflection On Affirmation (Write Here):

Step By Step

I Am Moving Towards

The Goals

And Achieve Success.

I Am Aligned

To The Universal Energy

And Manifesting

My Heart's Desires.

I Am Raising

My Vibrations

And Releasing Anything That Is Negative. I Am On Verge Of Achieving Good Health, Love, Wealth And Life I Always Dreamt About.

I Am Blessed With Divine Synchronicity And Healing While Rooted To Mother Earth.

Reflection On Affirmation (Write Here):

I Rise With The New Hope.

I Imbibe

That Hope Within Me

With The Gratitude

Towards Nature

 For Providing Me

All I Need.

I Call Upon

My Powers To Heal

And Achieve Abundance.

I Manifest

My Desires With Ease.

Reflection On Affirmation (Write Here):

I Am Living My Dream.

I Am Ready

To Receive Love

And Abundance In My Life.

I Am Aligned

With The Universe

And Manifest My Desires.

I Am Receiving

The Gifts

From The Universe.

I Am Ready.

Reflection On Affirmation (Write Here):

I Rise With Love

And Gratitude

In My Heart.

I Can See The Beauty

In Every Life Form

In The Universe.

I Am Thankful

To The Universe

For All The Learnings

And Gifts.

I Am Manifesting

My Hearts Desires Effortlessly With My Conscious Mind and Greater Connection With Mother Earth.

I Am Ready.

Reflection On Affirmation (Write Here):

When Everything

Happens In Now.

I Accept

And Embrace The Now.

In The Journey Of Life

I Whole Heartedly Embrace

The Present

And Manifest

My Desires With Ease.

Reflection On Affirmation (Write Here):

I Accept

And Embrace

The Divine Timing

For My Miracles.

I Am Perfectly Aligned

With The Universe

To Manifest

My Dreams With Ease.

I Am Receiving Abundance

From Every Direction

With Ease.

I Am Awakened And Ready.

Reflection On Affirmation (Write Here):

I Am Filled With Love

And Passion

For A Beautiful Life.

I Am Blessed With Love

And Abundance

For A Successful Life.

I Am Cared With Love

And Good Health

For A Meritorious Life.

I Am Centred With Love

And Observation For A Mindful Life. I Am Healed With Love And Courage For A Deserving Life.

Reflection On Affirmation (Write Here):

I Claim My Purpose Of Life

And Root Self

To Mother Earth

Creating The World

Filled With

Love And Hope.

I Manifest

My Hearts Desires

With Ease

As Money Flows

To Me With Ease. I Take My Position As The Universal Energy Flows Through Me Creating Life And In Complete Universal Alignment.

Reflection On Affirmation (Write Here):

I Can Feel The Universal Energy

Flow Through My Chakras

And Activating Them,

As I Get Closer To

The True Purpose

Of My Life

Gaining

The Power Of Creation.

I Am Manifesting Love,

Health, Wealth And World

Filled With Peace And Empathy.

Reflection On Affirmation (Write Here):

I Can Feel

The Unlocking

And Unblocking

Of The True Power

That Resides

Deep Within Me,

Guided By The Divine

Connecting Me

To The Universe

As I Create

An Environment Of Eternal Love.

Reflection On Affirmation (Write Here):

Each Day

I Heal

From The Past Trauma

And Negative Experiences

Towards

The True Purpose

Of My Life,

As I Am Manifesting

My Life's Purpose

With True Love,

Care, Blessings, Abundance, Health, Wealth And Creation.

Reflection On Affirmation (Write Here):

Dear Universe!

I Am Ready

To Receive My Gifts.

I Am Deeply Rooted

With Mother Earth

and Nurture.

I Am Blessed

With Love, Finances,

Health And Abundance.

I Am On My Way

To My Destiny

And Life's Purpose.

I Am Manifesting My Hearts Desires Effortlessly.

Reflection On Affirmation (Write Here):

I Am Healing,

I Am Powerful,

I Am Grateful,

I Am Manifesting,

I Am Abundant,

I Am Divine,

I Am Purposeful,

I Am Rooted,

I Am Loved,

I Am Cared,

I Am Blessed,

I Am Awakened,

I Am! I Am! I Am!

Reflection On Affirmation (Write Here):

I Am Grateful

For The Beautiful Life

And Each Day

I Am Realising

My True Powers.

As I Am Releasing

All The Blockages

And Giving Me

The Purpose

Towards A Life

With Love, Care, Health, Blessings, Abundance And Connection.

Reflection On Affirmation (Write Here):

I Believe

And Rise

With The New Hope,

Power And Miracle

To Manifest In My Life.

I Am Receiving Abundance

From Every Direction

With Ease.

I Am Aligned

With The Universe

And Receiving Love, Finances, Health, Happiness

And Strength To Serve Humanity.

Reflection On Affirmation (Write Here):

I Open

Myself

To All Goodness

In The Universe

And Receive It.

I Am Ready

To Receive

All The Prosperity

And Achievements

I Am Destined For.

It Is My Time.

Reflection On Affirmation (Write Here):

As The Cycle Of Time Moves On

It Is The New Year

With New Beginnings

And Possibilities.

I Therefore Claim

All My Possibilities

With A Fresh Mindset

Of Deeper Understanding

And Abundance.

I Have Shun

All The Darkness To Allow The Light To Enter And Guide Me Towards The Ultimate Purpose With Good Health, Love, Wealth, Deeper Connections For Greater Achievements.

Reflection On Affirmation (Write Here):

 I Am The Miracle

I Always Wanted.

I Am Manifesting

My Dreams

Without Any Effect

Of The Circumstances

Around Me.

I Am Deeply Rooted

With Mother Earth

and Nurtured.

I Am Blessed

With Love, Happiness, Health, Wealth And Peace.

I Am Ready.

Reflection On Affirmation (Write Here):

I Am Right

On My Path

To My Destiny.

I Am Completely

Supported By The Universe

And People Around Me

To Achieve It.

I Am Easily

Manifesting My Desires

With My Conscious Mind.

 I Am Operating

From My Highest Vibration Of Love And Creativity.

I Am Ready For My Miracles.

Reflection On Affirmation (Write Here):

With An Open Heart

I Am Open

To Receive,

Today I Will Receive

Returns

Of My Hard Work!!!!!

Reflection On Affirmation (Write Here):

I Am Operating

At The Highest Vibration.

I Am Aligned

With The Universe

And Receiving Abundance.

I Am Easily Manifesting

My Desires With Ease

Through My Conscious Mind.

I Am Ready

To Receive My Gifts

From The Universe.

I Own The Positive Energy Around Me.

Reflection On Affirmation (Write Here):

Today!

I Enter The Circle

Of Everlasting

Good Fortune

And Abundance!

Reflection On Affirmation (Write Here):

I Unblock

All That Is Block

And Prepare Myself

For The Abundance

 I Am Born To Receive.

I Align With The Universe

And Manifest

My Desires With Ease

Through

 My Conscious Mind.

I Am Peaceful And My Heart Is Filled With Gratitude Towards All.

I Am Unlocking My Powers And Claiming Them.

Reflection On Affirmation (Write Here):

I Am

Having Abundance In Life.

I Have

All The Money I Need.

I Am Super fit.

My Business

Is Growing Fast.

I Have Found

Love Of My Life.

All My Dreams

Have Come True.

Reflection On Affirmation (Write Here):

The Universe

Is Reciprocating

My Trust

And Giving Me

The Results

Of My Endeavours.

Reflection On Affirmation (Write Here):

The Universal Energy

Is Flowing

Through Me

And Guiding Me

Towards Abundance

In My Life.

Reflection On Affirmation (Write Here):

I Am Awake

With Love

And Gratitude

For All.

I Am Aligned

With The Universe.

I Am Manifesting

My Hearts Desires

Effortlessly

With My Conscious Mind.

I Am Abundant.

I Have Overcome My Fears To Rise To My Destiny.

Reflection On Affirmation (Write Here):

The Power

Of Universal Energy

Surrounds Me

And Heals Me,

Leading To

Easy Flow Of Money

And Abundance.

Reflection On Affirmation (Write Here):

The Golden Rays

 Of Rising Sun

Reach Me

With The Power Of Light

And Life.

They Have Removed

Every Inch Of Darkness,

Fear And Blocks

That Restricted My Growth.

I Am Now Connected Deeply

With The Mother Nature And Universal Energy Bringing Me Peace, Love, Health, Wealth And Abundance In Every Aspect Of My Life.

Reflection On Affirmation (Write Here):

I Trust The Process

And Know

It Is Time

For Me

To Rise

To My Highest Level.

Reflection On Affirmation (Write Here):

I Am Well Protected

From Anything

And Anyone

Wishing For My Bad.

I Am Building Strength

From My Core

With Deeper Connection

To The Universal Energy

Building

A Protection

From All Evil.

Reflection On Affirmation (Write Here):

The Challenges I Have

Are Meant

To Strengthen Me

And Make Me

A Stronger Version

Of Self.

Each Moment

I Am Blessed

And Well Protected

By The Divine.

Reflection On Affirmation (Write Here):

I Am Ready

For All My Gifts

Dear Universe.

I Am Working

From

My Highest Potential.

I Am Attracting Love,

Happiness, Health,

Abundance And Peace.

I Am Deeply Rooted

With Mother Earth.

I Am Healed And Contributing My Bit To Universal Healing.

Reflection On Affirmation (Write Here):

I Am At Peace

With Self

And

In Complete Alignment

With Universal Energy

To Manifest

My Desires

And

Experience The Miracles.

Reflection On Affirmation (Write Here):

With Faith

In Universal Plan,

I Accept My Calling

And Enter The Process

Which Guides Me

To The Purpose

I Was Born To Fulfil.

Reflection On Affirmation (Write Here):

I Am Centred

With Complete Control

On My Thoughts.

I Am Aligned

With The Universe

And Receiving Abundance

In Every Aspect Of My Life.

I Am Evolving

Towards My Best Version

Every Day.

I Am Ready To Manifest

All My Miracles With My Conscious Mind.

Reflection On Affirmation (Write Here):

I Am Blessed With Divinity.

I Am Deeply Rooted

With Mother Earth.

I Am On My Way

To My Destiny.

Each Day

I Am Manifesting

My Hearts Desires

Effortlessly.

Reflection On Affirmation (Write Here):

I Choose Love

And Gratitude

In My Life.

I Manifest

My Heart's Desires

Effortlessly.

I Am Deeply Rooted

With Mother Earth

and Nurtured.

I Am Abundant.

Reflection On Affirmation (Write Here):

I Am Thankful

For The Beautiful Life.

I Am Thankful

For The Beautiful People

Around Me

With Beautiful Souls.

I Am Thankful

For The Strength

To Fight My Battles.

I Am Thankful

For The Love I Am Receiving. I Am Thankful For A Purposeful Life.

Thank You Dear Universe For All The Goodness Around Me.

Reflection On Affirmation (Write Here):

I Choose Healing

By Release The Anxiety,

Fear Of Uncertainty,

Removing The Blocks

In Receiving

Positive Energy

And Releasing

The Negative Energy

In The Form Of

Negative Thoughts

While Filling The Heart With Belief And Love To Manifest My Heart's Desires With Ease And Effortless Gain In Abundance At Every Aspect Of My Life.

Reflection On Affirmation (Write Here):

I Am Loved.

I Am Fit.

I Am Strong.

I Am Abundant.

I Am Attracting

Effortlessly Money

Into My Life.

I Am Manifesting

My Desires Immediately.

I Am Healed.

I Am Peaceful.

Reflection On Affirmation (Write Here):

The Miracles Have Started

To Appear

With The Vanishing

Of Struggles.

I Am Aligned

With The Divine Light

Manifesting Love, Health,

Wealth, And

Everlasting Abundance

With Inner Peace.

Reflection On Affirmation (Write Here):

I Am Flowing

Like The River

Making My Own Ways

Towards

The Beautiful Life

While

I Attract Good Health,

Wealth, Love,

Abundance, Blessings

And Inner Peace.

Reflection On Affirmation (Write Here):

My Efforts

Are Giving Results

Immediately

With The Blessings

Of The Divine.

Each Effort Brings

Multiplied Results

In My Favour

Giving Me

Everlasting Abundance.

Reflection On Affirmation (Write Here):

I Claim My Energies

And Clear Any Blocks

For Unstoppable

Abundance

While I Manifest Love,

Health, Wealth, Blessings

And Every Aspect

Of My Life.

Reflection On Affirmation (Write Here):

My Heart Is Filled

With Gratitude

And Love.

I Receive And Accept

The Positive Energies

Raising My Vibration

With Manifestation

Of Love,

Health, Wealth,

Blessings And Abundance

In Every Aspect Of My Life.

Reflection On Affirmation (Write Here):

I Have Found The Clarity

Through

The Purpose Of My Life.

Now, I Take The Centre Stage

Of All Creation

By Allowing

The Universal Energy

Of Creation

To Flow Through Me.

I Manifest Love, Health,

Wealth, Blessings And Abundance With Free Flow Even When I Am Not Working For Them.

Reflection On Affirmation (Write Here):

I Am Aligned

With The Free Flowing

Universal Energy

While

Raising My Vibrations

And Becoming

The Centre Of Creation,

Manifesting Dreams,

Love, Health,

Wealth, And Prosperity

 In All I Do.

Reflection On Affirmation (Write Here):

I Achieve

What I Put My Thoughts

And Hard Work Into.

I Am The Centre

Of The Universal Energy.

I Allow It To Create

The Greatest Reality

Of My Life.

I Am Firmly Supported,

Loved, Cared

And Blessed.

I Am Aligned. I Am Abundant.

Reflection On Affirmation (Write Here):

I Am Loved

And Am Operating

From

The Position Of Love

Spreading Love

And Healing.

My Heart Is Filled

With Gratitude

Sharing The Vibrations

Of Love ,

Raising My Vibrations. I Am Manifesting Everything I Desire With Ease

And They Are Coming To Me Even When I Am Sleeping.

Reflection On Affirmation (Write Here):

I Am At Peace With Myself

Working Towards

My Life's Purpose.

I Am Attracting Love,

Health, Wealth

And Greatness

I Am Born To Have.

I Am Constantly Raising

My Vibrations

Matching The Universal Energy

To Create

Positive Transformation.

Reflection On Affirmation (Write Here):

It May Not Be Visible

But My Growth Is On.

I Have Learned To Flow

With The Universal Energy

Without Limiting Myself

To Any Expectation

Or Predetermined Time.

I Trust The Process,

For Everything

Will Take Place

At Right Moment.

Reflection On Affirmation (Write Here):

Today I Release Everyone

And Everything

That Brings Negativity

And Drains My Energy.

Also, I Release

Those Memories

That Build Load

And Restrict My Thoughts

And My Abundance.

I Release Everything

That No Longer Serves Me.

I Release All The Blocks

To Start Afresh With All New Me

With Greater Power And Higher Determination Towards My Destiny.

I Am Ready!

Reflection On Affirmation (Write Here):

I Align My Karma

With

The Universal Energy Flow

Towards The Best For All

While I Manifest Love,

Health, Wealth,

Peace And Abundance

With Fulfilment

Of My Life's Purpose.

Reflection On Affirmation (Write Here):

Release! Release! Release!

That No Longer Serves You

In Your Life's Purpose.

Release!

The Negative Thoughts

And Negative Energies

 Around You

In Its Every Form.

Breathe In The Faith

And Hope

Bringing Abundance Of Positivity That Lightens Up Your Life At Every Levels.

Reflection On Affirmation (Write Here):

Power In Me Foundation is the publisher for this book "*55 Affirmations With Self Help Activities*" and the author is life coach "*Manoj Kumar Singh*".

As the name suggest, it is a Trust (NGO) working for the noble cause of creating awareness about rare diseases and helping people with rare conditions lead a dignified life.

The Power In Me Foundation is working on the sustainable development model, where it believes that the trust should give our services to raise the funds for its social activities. This way it can also develop a right environment for people with rare diseases and other disabilities for their empowerment.

Rare diseases are genetic in nature and in most cases have no treatment or in few cases very costly treatment that goes on for lifespan. The patient and family suffer mentally, socially, physically and financially due to these diseases forcing them to lead a life of misery. A positive awareness in the society will help alleviate their pain and give them the right to dignified life they deserve.

Book publishing is one way to help creative talents reach their target readers and even empower people with any disability with writing skills to start their income without any pressure. The part of the amount collected through publishing and selling of the book is saved for the fulfilment of the objectives of the Trust. Further the donations and this fund will be used to set up training facilities, schools, academies, colleges, treatment centres and scholarships for the disables and people with rare diseases.

Ruh-E-Mohabbat is a creative wing of Power In Me Foundation that focuses on exploring the creativity for cause. It is a unique platform for anything creative and strives to help budding talents by giving them exposure.

You can contact us at mpowerinme@gmail.com for supporting our cause through donations or for any publishing services that you may need. You can even sponsor open mics or similar events that are organized by our creative wing. You can also call or WhatsApp at +918851537816.